W9-ASB-838

CONTENTS

❦ Lake Classic Short Stories ❧

*"The universe is made of
stories, not atoms."*

—Muriel Rukeyser

"The story's about you."

—Horace

Everyone loves a good story. It is hard
to think of a friendlier introduction to
classic literature. For one thing, short
stories are *short*—quick to get into and
easy to finish. Of all the literary forms,
the short story is the least intimidating
and the most approachable.

Great literature is an important part
of our human heritage. In the belief that
this heritage belongs to everyone, *Lake
Classic Short Stories* are adapted for
today's readers. Lengthy sentences and
paragraphs are shortened. Archaic words
are replaced. Modern punctuation and
spellings are used. Many of the longer
stories are abridged. In all the stories,

5

painstaking care has been taken to preserve the author's unique voice.

Lake Classic Short Stories have something for everyone. The hundreds of stories in the collection cover a broad terrain of themes, story types, and styles. Literary merit was a deciding factor in story selection. But no story was included unless it was as enjoyable as it was instructive. And special priority was given to stories that shine light on the human condition.

Each book in the *Lake Classic Short Stories* is devoted to the work of a single author. Little-known stories of merit are included with famous old favorites. Taken as a whole, the collected authors and stories make up a rich and diverse sampler of the story-teller's art.

Lake Classic Short Stories guarantee a great reading experience. Readers who look for common interests, concerns, and experiences are sure to find them. Readers who bring their own gifts of perception and appreciation to the stories will be doubly rewarded.

❧ Anton Chekhov ❧
(1860–1904)

About the Author

Anton Chekhov was born in Taganrog, Russia. His father, a former serf, ran a general store. In later years Chekhov would describe him as a "dishonest, domineering man—who nevertheless was eager to impart his love for music and art to his children."

The Chekhovs were a lively and clever family. Anton and his two brothers were artists. Two of them began writing comic stories in their college years. The third brother drew cartoons.

Chekhov trained as a physician at Moscow University. But he practiced very little as a doctor. He had already begun to sell short pieces to humor magazines while still in medical school. Soon he became successful enough to write as he pleased. It was then that he began the serious work that made his worldwide reputation.

Much of Chekhov's work focused on the sadness, or melancholy, of life. He once said, "Melancholy is to the Russian writer what the potato is to a French chef: it can be dished out in a hundred different ways."

Chekhov's first love was for the theater. His great plays *The Seagull, Uncle Vanya, The Cherry Orchard,* and *The Three Sisters* established him as one of the greatest dramatists of modern times. In 1901 he married Olga Knipper, the young actress who played leading parts in his plays.

Chekhov wrote hundreds of short stories and novellas. These works have had an enormous influence on the art of fiction.

Just three years after his marriage, Chekhov died of tuberculosis while visiting Germany. In tribute to his humanity and the responsibility of his work, Tolstoy called him "an artist of life."

The Bet

Two men at a party have an argument. They make a high-stakes bet to settle the matter. How much would *you* risk to prove your point? Would you bet your life?

"I BET YOU TWO MILLION THAT YOU WOULDN'T LAST FIVE
YEARS IN A PRISON CELL!"

The Bet

I

It was a dark fall night. An elderly banker was walking back and forth across the floor of his study. He was thinking about a party that he had given one fall 15 years ago. Many clever people had come, and the company had been most interesting. Among other things, they had talked about capital punishment. Should a person be put to death for commiting a terrible crime? That was the question.

Most of the guests had been against it. In their eyes this form of punishment was old-fashioned. It went against all their ideas of right and wrong. They said it was not fit for civilized states. Some thought that the death penalty should be replaced everywhere by a sentence of life in prison.

"I don't agree," the banker had told his guests. "I've never tasted capital punishment or life in prison myself. But if I may offer my thoughts, I think that capital punishment is kinder than a life in jail. The death penalty would kill you right away. A life in prison does it slowly. Which sentence shows more kindness? One that takes just a few minutes to kill you? Or one that drags the life out of you over many years?"

"Both are wrong," said one of the guests. "Both have the same purpose—to take life. But the state isn't God. The state can't *give* life. So it has no right to take it away!"

Among the guests was a young lawyer who was about 25 years old. When asked for his thoughts he said, "The death penalty and life in prison are *both* wrong. But if I had to choose between death or prison for life, I would choose the second. I am sure of it. Any sort of life is better than no life at all."

A lively argument had broken out then. The banker was younger and more excitable in those days. Now he suddenly got angry. He banged his fist on the table. He shouted at the young lawyer. "That's not true! I bet you two million that you wouldn't even last five years in a prison cell."

"Do you really mean that?" the lawyer asked. "Then I bet you I could stay locked up for *fifteen* years, not five."

"Fifteen? Done!" shouted the banker.

"I bet two million on it!"

"I accept! You're betting millions. I'm betting my freedom!" the lawyer said.

And so that senseless bet was made. The banker was a spoiled man at that time. He had more millions than he could count and often wasted his money. Over supper he made fun of the lawyer. "Come to your senses, young man, before it's too late," he said. "Two million is chicken-feed to me. You, however, could lose three or four of the best years of your life. I say three or four because you won't last longer.

"And remember this, poor man. Being held in jail *by choice* is much harder than being held against your will. The thought that you could be free any minute will eat away at you in your prison. I feel sorry for you!"

As the banker walked back and forth across his room, he now remembered all of what had been said.

"What was the point of that bet?" he wondered. "What was the use of that lawyer losing 15 years of his life? Why would I throw away two million? How could that prove that the death penalty is any better or worse than life in prison? It's completely mad! On my part it was the fancy of someone with far too much money. On the lawyer's part, it was pure greed!"

A little while later he remembered everything else that happened that evening. They had decided upon where the lawyer must serve his time. It would be in one of the small houses in the banker's garden. The lawyer would be always under guard.

These were the rules: For 15 years he was not to cross the doorway. He would not see a living person, hear another voice, or get newspapers or letters. He could have a musical instrument and books to read. He could write letters, drink wine, and smoke. But he would not be allowed to speak one word. Instead, there would be a small, specially built window through which he could pass little notes. He would be completely alone.

The lawyer would serve a term of *exactly* 15 years—from 12 o'clock on November 14, 1870, until 12 o'clock on November 14, 1885. The lawyer must not try to break any rule. If he did, even two minutes before the time was up, the banker would not have to pay the two million to him.

During his first year in the prison, the lawyer was very lonely and bored. At least as far as one could tell in his short notes. Day and night the sound of a piano came from the little house. He refused to smoke or drink wine. Wine, he said, made him long for things he could not have. Besides, it was sad to drink good wine alone. Smoking, he wrote, would ruin the air in his room. For the first year the lawyer mainly had light books sent in. He read love stories, funny stories, and mysteries.

In the second year, music could no longer be heard from the little house. The lawyer wrote and asked for the world's most famous books. In the fifth year, music was heard again and the prisoner asked for wine. People watching him through the window all said the same thing. For the whole year, he did nothing but eat, drink, and lie upon his bed. Sometimes he yawned and talked angrily to himself, but he didn't read any books. Often he would sit up writing all night. But toward the morning, he would tear up everything he had written. More than once they heard him crying.

In the second half of the sixth year, the

prisoner turned to the study of languages and history. He studied so hard that the banker had a hard time getting all the books he wanted. Over four years, nearly 600 books had been brought to him. During this time the banker happened to receive the following letter from his prisoner:

My dear Jailer:

I'm writing these lines in six languages. Have them checked over. If there are no mistakes, I beg you to have a shot fired in the garden. That will prove to me that my work has not been for nothing. The wisest people of all times and in all countries speak different languages. But the same flame burns in all of them. If only you knew the joy I feel in my heart now that I can understand them!

The prisoner's wish was carried out. The banker ordered a shot to be fired in the garden.

After the tenth year the lawyer sat without moving at his table. He read nothing but the Bible. Then the Bible was followed by the history of religion.

During the last two years, the prisoner read a huge number of books. He read anything and everything. First he read natural science. Then he asked for the plays of Shakespeare. In some of his notes he asked for books on chemistry, medicine, or more stories. He wanted them all at the same time. His reading made one think of someone swimming in the sea with his broken ship all around him. To save his life, the swimmer was grabbing at one piece of wood after another.

II

As he remembered all this, the old banker thought, "Tomorrow at 12 o'clock he goes free. I shall have to pay him two million. But if I pay up—I'm finished. I'll be completely ruined."

Fifteen years ago the banker had more millions than he could count. Now they were nearly gone. He had gambled. He'd lost money in the stock market. Always he had wasted money without thinking. Once he had been a fearless, proud man with great riches. Now he worried over every mark in his bank book.

"That bet!" the old man growled. He held his head in his hands. "Why couldn't the man die? He's only just 40. He will take all my money. He'll marry, he'll enjoy life, he'll play the stock market. Meanwhile, I will live like a beggar. Every day I'll hear him say the same thing. 'I owe my happiness to you. Please let me help you.' No, it's too much! There is only one thing that can save me from losing everything. That man must die!"

Three o'clock struck. The banker listened. The whole household was sleeping. The only sound was the wind in the frozen trees outside. Trying not to make any noise, he took a key from his safe. It would unlock the door that had been closed tight for 15 years. He put on his coat and went out.

It was dark and cold outside, and it was raining. A sharp, wet wind howled around the whole garden. The banker couldn't see the ground, the little house, or the trees. As he neared the spot where the little house stood, he called out twice to his watchman. There was no reply. The fellow was probably hiding out from the weather. He must be fast asleep in the kitchen or the greenhouse.

"I must be brave enough to carry out my plan," thought the old man. "No one will blame me. People will most likely think that the watchman did it."

By feeling about in the dark, he found the steps and the door. He felt his way into a small hall and lit a match. No one was there. The seals on the door leading to the prisoner's room had not been broken.

When the match went out, the old man peeked through the small window. He was shaking with excitement.

In the prisoner's room one candle burned. The lawyer was sitting at the table. Only his back, the hair on his head, and his hands could be seen. Open books lay on the table, on two chairs, and on the rug near the table.

Five minutes passed without the prisoner moving. His 15 years in a jail had taught him to sit still. The banker tapped on the window with one finger. The prisoner did not move. The banker carefully broke the seals on the doors. He put the key in the keyhole. The old lock squeaked and the door creaked. The banker waited to hear a shout of surprise. Three minutes went by and it was still quiet on the other side. The old banker decided to go in.

A man quite different than any normal human being was sitting at the table. He did not move. The man was all skin and bones and he had the long, curly hair of a woman. His skin was yellow, his cheeks were hollow, and he had a shaggy beard. The hand that held up his bushy head was so thin and wasted that it was sad to look at. His hair was already touched with gray. No one looking at that lined, tired face would have believed that he was only 40. He was sleeping. A sheet of paper lay on the table in front of his bowed head. Something was written on it in small letters.

"Poor man!" thought the banker. "He's asleep and probably dreaming of those millions! All I have to do is take hold of this half-dead body and throw it on the bed. I'll just gently hold a pillow over his face. There won't be any sign of murder. But first, let me read the letter he has written."

The banker picked up the paper. He read the following:

Tomorrow at 12 o'clock I will be free. I will have the right to mix with people again. But there is something that I must do before I leave this room and see the sun once more. There are some things I feel I should tell you. With a clear mind and before God, I declare that I hate freedom, life, and health. I hate everything that those books of yours call the blessings of this world.

I have spent 15 years making a careful study of life on earth. True, I haven't seen anything of the earth or of people. But in your books I have sung songs, hunted deer in the forest, loved women. Beautiful creatures made by the magic of your great poets have visited me at night. They have whispered stories in my ear that made my head spin.

In my readings I have climbed mountains. From their tops I have seen the sun rise in the morning and paint the sky with red-gold in the evening. I have seen the lightning flash above me. I have seen forests, fields, rivers, lakes, towns. In your books I have thrown myself into deep pits. I have murdered, burned cities, and won entire kingdoms.

Your books have made me wise. The learning of all the ages is held in a tiny lump inside my head. I know more than you can ever imagine.

And I hate your books. I hate all the blessings of this world. Everything is without worth, and all that beauty is just a trick. Nothing lasts for more than a moment. You may be proud, wise, and handsome. But death will wipe all of you from the face of the earth. You will be as dead as the mice under the floorboards. Those who came before you and those who come after you end as nothing but dust.

You've lost all reason and are on the wrong path. You mistake lies for truth and the ugly for the beautiful. You would be surprised if apple trees suddenly started growing frogs instead of fruit. You would be amazed if roses smelled like sweaty horses. You people have traded heaven for earth. I just don't want to understand you.

To show how much I hate what you live by, I refuse the two million. I once dreamed of the millions as though they were heaven. But now I feel only hate for them. To give up my right to them, I shall leave this place five hours before the set time. Thus I shall lose the bet.

After reading this, the banker laid the paper on the table. He kissed the strange man's head. Then, crying, he left the little house. At no other time, not even after heavy losses in the stock market, had he hated himself more than now. Back in his house, he went to bed. But excitement and tears kept him awake for a long time.

Next morning a white-faced watchman came running in to tell the news. They had seen the man from the little house climb through his window into the garden. He had run for the gate and then disappeared.

The banker went to the little house

with his servants. He had to make certain that the prisoner had, in fact, fled. He picked up the paper that the lawyer had written. To make sure that there would be no questions later on, he returned to the house and locked it in his safe.

Gooseberries

What symbolizes success for you? The ambitious man in this story knows exactly what he wants. He gives up everything else to achieve his dream. Do you think he pays too high a price? Read to decide.

My brother was now a landowner. He forgot that our grandfather had been a peasant.

Gooseberries

The sky had been gray since early morning. It was a still day—not hot, but tiring. It was the kind of day when clouds hang over the fields, and you wait for rain that does not come. Ivan Ivanych, an animal doctor, and Burkin, a high school teacher, were already tired from walking. The broad plain seemed to have no end.

Far ahead they could just see the windmills of the village. To the right lay hills in the distance beyond the village. Both of them knew what was over there.

31

There were the river, and fields, green trees, and homes. If you stood on one of the hills, you could see another wide plain, telegraph poles, and a train that looked like a snake crawling. In clear weather you could even see the town.

Now it was still. Nature itself seemed quiet and full of thought. Ivan Ivanych and Burkin were filled with love for this plain. Both of them were thinking what a beautiful land it was.

"The other day," said Burkin, "you were going to tell me a story."

"Yes, I wanted to tell you about my brother."

Ivan Ivanych breathed a slow sigh. He lit his pipe before beginning his story. But just then it began to rain. Five minutes later it was pouring so hard that they couldn't tell when the rain would end. The two men stopped. They were not sure what to do. The dogs that walked

with them were already wet. Now they
stood with their tails between their legs.
They looked at the men.

"We must find cover somewhere," said
Burkin. "Let's go to Alyohin's. It's quite
near."

"Let's."

They turned aside and walked across
a freshly cut meadow. They walked
straight ahead, and then to the right,
until they reached the road. Soon tall,
slender trees came into view. They saw
a garden, then the red roofs of barns. The
view opened on a broad river with a mill
and a white bathing-cabin. That was
Alyohin's place.

The mill was going, drowning out the
sound of the rain. Wet horses stood near
the carts, their heads down. Men were
walking about, their heads covered with
bags. It was damp and muddy, and the
water looked cold. Ivan Ivanych and

Burkin felt cold and uncomfortable through and through. Their feet were heavy with mud. When they climbed up to the barns, they were silent as though they were angry at each other.

The noise of a machine came from one of the barns. The door was open, and clouds of dust were pouring out. In the doorway stood Alyohin himself. He was a man of 40, tall and round, with long hair. Standing there, he looked more like a teacher or an artist than a gentleman farmer. He was wearing a loose white shirt, badly in need of washing. It was belted with a rope. His pants and his high boots were thick with mud and straw. His eyes and nose were black with dust. He greeted Ivan Ivanych and Burkin and seemed very glad to see them.

"Please go up to the house, gentlemen," he said, smiling. "I'll be there right away."

It was a large house of two stories. Alyohin lived downstairs in what had once been the servant's rooms. The furniture was plain. The place smelled of rye bread and saddle leather. Alyohin went into the finer rooms upstairs only when he had guests. Once in the house, the two visitors were met by a maid. The young woman was so beautiful that both of them stood still at the same moment. They looked at each other.

"You can't imagine how glad I am to see you, gentlemen," said Alyohin as he joined them in the hall. "What a surprise!" Then he turned to the maid. "Give the guests a change of clothes," he said. "And, come to think of it, I will change, too. But first I must go and bathe. I don't think I've had a wash since spring. Don't you want to go into the bathing-cabin? In the meantime, things will be got ready here."

The beautiful maid, in her soft, sweet way, brought them bath towels and soap. Alyohin went to the bathing-cabin with his guests.

"Yes, it's been a long time since I've bathed," he said as he undressed. "I have a fine bathing-cabin, as you see. It was put up by my father. But somehow I never find time to use it." He sat down on the steps and soaped his long hair and neck. The water around him turned brown. "I haven't had a wash for a long time," Alyohin said again, as if to explain. He soaped himself once more. The water about him started to turn dark blue, the color of ink.

Ivan Ivanych came out of the cabin. He jumped into the river with a splash and swam in the rain. He held his arms out wide, raising waves. Then he swam out to the middle of the river and dived. A minute later he came up in another spot and swam on.

Ivan Ivanych kept diving, trying to reach the bottom. "By God!" he said again and again happily. "By God!" He swam to the mill, spoke to the peasants there, and turned back. Then, in the middle of the river, he lay floating, his face turned up to the rain. Burkin and Alyohin were already dressed and ready to leave. But Ivan Ivanych continued to swim and dive. "By God!" he kept shouting.

"You've had enough!" Burkin yelled to him.

They returned to the house. Soon the lamp was lit in the big room upstairs. The two guests, in silk robes and warm slippers, were resting in soft chairs. Alyohin himself was washed, combed, and wearing a new jacket. He walked about the room, seeming happy with his warm, clean, dry clothes.

Then the pretty maid stepped silently across the carpet. Smiling, she brought in a tray with tea. Only then did Ivan

Ivanych begin his story. It was as though not only Burkin and Alyohin were listening, but also the pictures on the walls. These pictures of fine ladies and soldiers looked down upon them calmly from their gold frames.

"We are two brothers," he began. "I, Ivan Ivanych, and my brother, Nikolay Ivanych, who is two years younger. I went to school to learn a profession. I became an animal doctor. Nikolay, at age 19, began to clerk in a branch of the Treasury. Our father was once a private in the military, but he rose to be an officer and a nobleman. He was able to leave us something when he died. But our father owed a lot of money. We had to use everything to pay his debts.

"As children, we lived in the country. Just like peasant children, we passed our days and nights in the fields and the woods. We herded horses, fished, and so on. We watched the birds fly south in the fall. Even now I feel like I do not belong in the town. On clear, cool days when birds sweep in flocks over the village, I have a longing for the open.

"My brother was unhappy working for the government. Years passed, but he went on warming the same seat. He scratched away at the same papers, thinking only of how to get away to the country. Little by little this longing turned into a dream. His dream was to buy his own land somewhere on the banks of a river or a lake.

"My brother Nikolay was a kind and gentle man and I loved him. But I never quite understood his wish. Why would a man want to shut himself up for the rest of his life on a little land of his own? It is a common saying that a man needs only six feet of earth. But six feet is what a dead body needs, not a man.

"It is also said that our educated class should go back to the country and settle on farms. Many people think that's a good thing. But these farms seem just like that same six feet of earth. To leave the city, to leave the struggle and the noise, to go off and hide on one's own farm—that's not life. It is selfishness, laziness. It is hiding away from the world like a monk, but without doing the good works of a monk. People do not need six feet of earth or a farm to be free. They need the whole globe, and all of nature.

"But my brother Nikolay sat in his office and dreamed of growing his own food. He dreamed of having picnics on green grass, sleeping in the sun, sitting for hours looking out at field and forest. Books on farming were his joy. He liked newspapers too. But he only read the advertisements of land for sale. In his mind, he pictured garden paths, flowers, fruit, bird-houses, ducks on the pond, and all that sort of thing, you know. These pictures that he imagined changed with the different advertisements. But somehow gooseberry bushes figured in every one of them. He could not picture to himself a single country-house without gooseberries.

"'There are great things about country life,' he used to say. 'You sit on the porch having tea while your ducks are swimming in the pond. Everything smells fresh—and the gooseberries are growing.'

"He would draw a plan of his place and it would always contain the following features: a) the master's house; b) the servants' quarters; c) kitchen garden; and d) a gooseberry patch. He never spent any money. He went without food and drink and dressed like a beggar. But he kept on saving money in the bank. He would not spend a cent. It hurt me to see it, and I used to send him money on holidays. But he would put that away too. Once a man is stuck on an idea, there is no doing anything with him.

"Years passed. Finally he was sent off to another branch to work. He was already past 40, yet he was still reading newspaper advertisements and saving up money. Then I heard that he was married. For the sake of buying land with a gooseberry patch, he married an older, rather plain woman. He did not love her at all. He married her simply because she had money.

"After his marriage, he still would not spend anything. He kept his wife hungry, and he put her money in the bank in his own name. The woman had once been the wife of a postmaster. He had treated her well and bought her cakes and pies. This second husband did not even give her enough bread. She became sick. Some three years later, she died. Of course, it never crossed my brother's mind that he was the cause of her death. Money can do strange things to a man.

"Once in our town, a shopkeeper lay dying. For his last meal, he ordered a plate of honey. He stirred up all of his money into the honey. Then he ate it so that no one should get it!

"On another day I was looking at a herd of cattle at a train station. I saw a cattle dealer fall under the train engine. It cut off his leg. We carried him to the hospital, the blood pouring from the man. It was a terrible thing! But he kept begging us to find his leg. For some reason he seemed very worried about it. We found out that he had money stuffed in the boot on that leg. He was afraid it would be lost."

"You've gone off on another story," said Burkin.

Ivan Ivanych stopped for a moment

and then went on with his story.

"After his wife's death, my brother began to look around for some land. Of course, you may look about for five years. In the end you may still buy the wrong place. You might buy something quite different from what you have been dreaming of.

"My brother bought some 300 acres of land. There was a house, servants' quarters, and a park on the land. But there was no duck pond and no gooseberry patch. There was a stream, but the water in it was the color of coffee. A glue factory was on one of its banks! But my brother was not bothered. He ordered some gooseberry bushes and planted them. Then he settled down to the life of a country gentleman.

"Last year I visited him. I thought I would go and see how things were. I reached his place in the afternoon. It was

LAKE CLASSICS

Great American Short Stories I

Washington Irving, Nathaniel Hawthorne, Mark Twain, Bret Harte, Edgar Allan Poe, Kate Chopin, Willa Cather, Sarah Orne Jewett, Sherwood Anderson, Charles W. Chesnutt

Great American Short Stories II

Herman Melville, Stephen Crane, Ambrose Bierce, Jack London, Edith Wharton, Charlotte Perkins Gilman, Frank R. Stockton, Hamlin Garland, O. Henry, Richard Harding Davis

Great British and Irish Short Stories I

Arthur Conan Doyle, Saki (H. H. Munro), Rudyard Kipling, Katherine Mansfield, Thomas Hardy, E. M. Forster, Robert Louis Stevenson, H. G. Wells, John Galsworthy, James Joyce

Great Short Stories from Around the World I

Guy de Maupassant, Anton Chekhov, Leo Tolstoy, Selma Lagerlöf, Alphonse Daudet, Mori Ogwai, Leopoldo Alas, Rabindranath Tagore, Fyodor Dostoevsky, Honoré de Balzac

Cover and Text Designer: Diann Abbott

Library of Congress Catalog Number: 94-075341
ISBN 1-56103-040-6
Printed in the United States of America
1 9 8 7 6 5 4 3 2

LAKE CLASSICS

Great Short Stories
from Around the World I

Anton
CHEKHOV

Stories retold by Joanne Suter
Illustrated by James McConnell

LAKE EDUCATION
Belmont, California

hot. I made my way to the house. There I was met by a fat dog. The dog had reddish hair and it looked something like a pig. The dog looked up, but it was too lazy to bark. The cook, a fat woman who also looked like a pig, came out of the kitchen. She said that the master was resting after dinner. I went in to see my brother and found him sitting up in bed with a blanket over his knees. He had grown older and heavier. His cheeks, his nose, his lips stuck out. It looked as though he might grunt into the blanket at any moment.

"We hugged. We cried with joy and sadness. At that moment it came to the two of us that we had once been young—but were now gray and nearing death. He got dressed and took me out to show me his land.

"'Well, how are you getting on here?' I asked him.

"'Oh, all right, thank God. I am doing very well.'

"He was no longer the poor, quiet clerk he used to be. Now he was a real landowner, a gentleman. He had already grown used to his new way of living. He ate a great deal, steamed himself in the bathhouse. He did no work and was growing fat.

"My brother told me that he was taking the glue factory to court. He said that it made him angry when the peasants forgot to address him as 'Your Honor.' He worried about going to heaven, he said, so he did good deeds. Of course, he did them in an upper-class manner—not simply, but with much show.

"On certain holidays he treated the peasants to a gallon of vodka. He thought this was a fine thing to do. Oh, those horrible gallons of vodka! One day a fat landowner calls the police because some peasants are crossing his land. The next day, to mark a holiday, he treats them to a gallon of vodka. The peasants drink and shout 'Hurrah.' When they are drunk, they bow down at his feet. It is no good for a peasant to have extra money, too much food, and too little to do. It makes a Russian think too highly of himself.

"When he was a government clerk, Nikolay Ivanych was afraid to have ideas of his own. Now he spoke as if his words were truths beyond question. 'Education is necessary, but the common people are not ready for it,' he explained. 'Many times it is wrong to give a beating as a punishment. But in some cases it is useful and nothing else will serve.'

"'I know the common people. I know how to deal with them,' he would say. 'They love me. I only have to raise my little finger, and they will do anything I want.'

"And all this, mark you, he would say with a smile. Some 20 times over he repeated, 'We, of the upper class,' and, 'I, as a landowner.' It seemed that he no longer remembered who we were. He had forgotten that our grandfather had been a peasant, and our father just a private.

"But now I want to talk not about him, but about me. A change took place in me during the few hours that I spent on his land. In the evening when we were having tea, the cook served a plate of gooseberries. They were not bought. They were my brother's own gooseberries—the first ones picked since the bushes were planted.

"My brother gave a laugh and then looked at the gooseberries in silence. There were tears in his eyes. He could not speak. Then he put one berry in his mouth. He looked like a child who had finally won a toy he had always wanted.

'Oh, how tasty!' he said as he ate the gooseberries greedily. 'Ah, how sweet! Do taste them!'

"The gooseberries were hard and sour. But remember what the famous author once wrote. He said that people would rather hear a lie that sings praises than hear a harsher truth. That evening I saw before me a happy man! I saw one whose dream had come true, who had reached his goal in life. The man before me had gotten what he wanted and was pleased with himself.

"For some reason, a bit of sadness had always been mixed with my thoughts about human happiness. Now, at the sight of a happy man, I was filled with a heavy, hopeless feeling. This feeling weighed on me most of that night. A bed was made up for me in a room next to my brother's room. I could hear that he was not asleep. He would get up again and again, go to the plate of gooseberries, and eat one after another.

"I said to myself, how many happy people there really are! What a powerful force they are! Look at life! So many of those who are strong stand above it all and do nothing. Yet there is horrible, grinding poverty everywhere. There is overcrowding and lying. And the children are even worse than their parents.

"Yet in all the houses and on all the streets there is peace and quiet. Of the 50,000 people who live in our town, there is not one who would cry out aloud. Not one who would let his angry voice be heard by others. We see the people who go to market, eat by day, sleep by night. They talk without meaning. They marry, grow old, and quietly drag their dead to the cemetery.

"But we do not see or hear those who suffer. What is terrible in life goes on somewhere behind the scenes. On the outside everything is peaceful and quiet. Only the numbers recorded in books silently speak the truth: so many people gone out of their minds, so many gallons of vodka drunk, so many children dead from hunger. . . .

"And such a state of things seems to be necessary. It appears that the happy man is at ease only because the unhappy ones carry their heavy loads in silence. And if there were not this silence, happiness would be impossible. It is a simple idea.

"Do you know what should be behind the door of every contented, happy man? There ought to be someone standing there with a little hammer. With a knock, the happy man should often be reminded that there are unhappy people. However happy he may be, life will sooner or later show him its claws. Trouble will come to him—illness, poverty, losses. When that happens, no one will see or hear him. Just as now the happy man neither sees nor hears those who suffer. But there is no man with a hammer. The happy man lives at his ease. He is faintly moved by small daily cares—as a leafy tree is moved by the wind—and all is well.

"That night I came to understand that I, too, had been contented and happy," Ivan Ivanych continued. He stood up. "I, too, always knew what to say over the dinner table or out hunting. I always had strong ideas on how to live, what to believe, and the right way to govern the people. I, too, would say that learning was the enemy of darkness. But then I'd say that, for the common people, the three R's were enough for the time being. Freedom is great, I used to say. We need it as much as air. But we must wait awhile. Yes, that's what I used to say.

"And now I ask, 'Why must we wait?'"
Ivan Ivanych looked angrily at Burkin.
"Why must we wait, I ask you? For what
reason? I am told that nothing can be
done all at once. Again and again I hear
that every idea takes time. But who is it
that says so?

"You say that is the law of nature, the
way of the world. But is there a law that
says that I—a living, thinking man—
should stand beside a ditch and wait for
it to fill itself up with dirt? Or should I
jump over it or throw a bridge across it?
Again, why must we wait? Shall we wait
until we have no strength to live? Yet we
have to live and want to live!

"I left my brother's place early in the
morning. Ever since then it has become
impossible for me to stay in town. I am
afraid to look at the windows of houses.
Nothing hurts me now more than seeing
a happy family having tea. I am an old

man now—too old to fight. I am not even able to hate. Now I can only feel sad inside, angry and worked up. But at night my head is on fire with a rush of ideas. I cannot go to sleep. Oh, if I were only young again!"

Ivan Ivanych walked quickly back and forth across the room. He said again, "If I were young!"

Suddenly he walked up to Alyohin and took his hands.

"Don't quiet down," he begged his friend. "Don't let yourself be put to sleep! As long as you are young, strong, and aware, do not stop doing good! There is no happiness and there should be none. If life has a meaning and a purpose, that meaning and purpose is not our happiness. It is something greater. Do good!"

All of this Ivan Ivanych said with a hopeful smile. It was as though he were asking something for himself.

Later, all three men sat in soft chairs in different corners of the big room. They were silent. Ivan Ivanych's story was not enough for either Burkin or Alyohin. After all, the ladies and soldiers were looking down from the gold frames. It seemed tiresome to listen to the story of a poor clerk who ate gooseberries. A man at rest felt like talking about fine people, about women. They were sitting in a lovely room with soft chairs and a thick carpet. Everything around them whispered that the beautiful people in the pictures had once moved about here. They had sat in this very room and drank tea. Now the lovely maid was quietly moving about. This was real. It was better than any story.

Alyohin was very sleepy. He had gotten up early to do his work. Now he could hardly keep his eyes open. But he was afraid his visitors might tell an interesting story. He tried to stay awake.

He did not bother to ask himself if what Ivan Ivanych had just said was right. The guests were not talking about something real like hay or oats. They were talking about something that had no direct bearing on his life. He was glad of it and wanted them to go on.

"I'm afraid it is my bedtime," said Burkin, standing. "Allow me to wish you good night."

So Alyohin, too, left his guests. He went downstairs to his own rooms, while they stayed upstairs. They were to sleep in two old wooden beds decorated with carvings. The wide, cool beds had been made up by the lovely maid. The bed coverings gave off a clean, fresh smell.

Ivan Ivanych undressed silently. He got into bed.

"Oh, Lord, forgive us sinners!" he whispered. Then he drew the blanket over his head.

His pipe, which lay on the table, smelled strongly of burned tobacco. Burkin could not sleep for a long time. He lay in bed wondering where the bad smell came from.

The rain beat against the window all night.

The Little Apples

Why would *anyone* find pleasure in humiliating others? In this story, the author paints a grim and haunting picture of a corrupt landowner. Read on to see how evil breeds evil.

"ARE YOU FRIGHTENED OF OLD KARPUSHKA? MOST
LIKELY HE'S OFF DRINKING SOMEWHERE."

The Little Apples

Near the Black Sea the landowner Trifon Semyonovich had been living on his own black earth for a long time. He owned about 8,000 acres of land. These holdings had been mortgaged and put up for sale. The "For Sale" notices were put up long ago—in the days before Trifon found himself with a bald spot. But the land had never been sold, thanks both to the bank manager's foolishness and to Trifon Semyonovich's tricks.

One day, of course, the bank will fail. This will happen because Trifon Semyonovich and many others take out bank loans without paying interest. Indeed, Semyonovich made a great show of it when he did pay a little interest on his loan. It was as if he was doing something great, like building a church.

If this world were not this world, and if things were called by a fitting name, then Trifon Semyonovich would be called by another name. He would be given a name usually used for a barnyard animal. Frankly, Trifon Semyonovich is nothing more than a beast. I am sure he would agree with me. If he ever hears of this, he will not be upset. He is quite a smart man and is likely to agree with the things I have said.

I shall not describe everything about Trifon Semyonovich. To describe him completely would mean writing a very thick book. I shall not talk about his cheating at cards. I shall not bring up the tricks he plays on the old priest. I shall keep to one story that shows his attitude toward his fellow creatures.

It was a perfectly beautiful morning at the end of a long summer. Trifon Semyonovich found himself walking down a long and narrow path in his beautiful orchard. The apples there were so fine that poets might write about them. Those apples seemed to say "Pick me! Pick me! Enjoy yourselves, for the fall will soon come!"

But Trifon Semyonovich was not enjoying himself that morning. This was, in part, because he was far from being a poet. But it was also because he had passed a very uncomfortable night. This always happened when he had lost a lot of money at cards.

Behind Trifon Semyonovich marched

his faithful servant Karpushka, a man
of about 60 years old. The man kept
looking quickly from side to side. A
description of Karpushka would be even
longer than a description of Trifon
Semyonovich. He did well at shining
boots, still better at hanging unwanted
dogs. He stole everything he could lay
his hands on and made a wonderfully
sneaky spy. Some peasants or neighbors
are always complaining about some
terrible thing that Karpushka has done.
But nothing ever comes of it. Trifon
Semyonovich rightly believes Karpushka
would be hard to replace.

When Trifon Semyonovich goes for a
walk, the trusty Karpushka always goes
with him. This way is safer and more
pleasant. Karpushka has a never-ending
supply of tall stories. He never stops
telling them. In fact, he never stops talking.

On this morning he was walking

behind his master and telling a long story. It was about two schoolboys wearing white caps. The boys had made their way into the orchard with sticks and arrows in their hands. They had begged him, Karpushka, to let them go hunting. They had even offered him money. But he was true to his master, as always. After turning away their offer, he had set the two dogs, Chestnut and Gray, on them.

Just as Karpushka finished his story, they heard a strange noise in a nearby clump of apple trees. Karpushka stopped talking and listened. Thinking that he knew that certain sound, he pulled at his master's coat. Then he hurried off as quickly as he could in the direction of the sound. Trifon Semyonovich was looking forward to some pleasant excitement. He hurried after Karpushka with an old man's tiny steps.

On the edge of the orchard, under an old spreading apple tree, stood a peasant girl. She was slowly chewing on an apple. Not far from her a strong, tall peasant boy crawled on his hands and knees. He was picking up apples that had fallen from the tree.

The boy tossed the green apples into the bushes. But the ripe ones were presented to his girlfriend in his strong and dirty hands. The girl kept chewing on the apples, one after another. The boy continued to pick them up, crawling over the ground. His mind was clearly on his girlfriend and no one else.

"Take an apple off the tree," the girl whispered.

"I wouldn't dare."

"What are you frightened of? Old Karpushka? Most likely he's off drinking somewhere."

The boy jumped up. He sprang into the

air and picked a single apple from the tree. He handed it to the girl. But like Adam and Eve in days of old, the boy and girl would pay dearly for their apple. She bit off a small piece of it. She gave this piece to the boy. But no sooner had they tasted the apple than they both turned white. It was not because the apple was bad. It was because they saw the frowning face of Trifon Semyonovich and Karpushka's little snout with its ugly, twisted smile.

"Good day to you, my dears," Trifon Semyonovich said. He came towards them. "So you're enjoying the little apples, eh? I hope I am not bothering you."

The boy took off his cap. His head hung low. The girl looked down at her apron.

"Well, Gregory, how are you these days?" Trifon Semyonovich went on, talking to the boy. "How are things going, lad?"

"I only took one," the boy whispered. "I picked it off the ground."

Trifon Semyonovich turned to the girl.

"How are you, my little darling?"

She found herself looking even more closely at her apron.

"Well, now, we haven't been to your wedding yet, have we?"

"No, sir, we haven't. I swear that we only took one apple. And that little apple wasn't even . . ."

He turned to the boy.

"Good, good. Fine fellow. Learned how to read yet?"

"No, sir. We only took one apple, sir, and we found it on the ground."

"You don't know how to read, but you do know how to steal, eh? When did you start stealing?"

"I wasn't stealing, sir."

"Then what about your pretty little sweetheart?" Karpushka broke in. He turned to the boy. "Why is she looking so unhappy? Is it because you are not showing her enough love?"

"Oh, shut up, Karpushka!" Trifon Semyonovich exclaimed. "Gregory, I want you to tell me a story."

Gregory coughed. He gave a strange smile.

"I don't know any stories, sir. I don't need your apples, either. When I want apples, I'll go and buy them!"

"It's a great joy to me that you are rich, my boy. But still—I want you to tell me a story. I will listen. Karpushka will listen. Your little sweetheart will listen, too. Don't be afraid. Be brave. 'Brave is the heart of a thief.' Isn't that a true saying, my dear fellow?"

Trifon Semyonovich let his eyes rest on the boy, who had fallen into the trap. Sweat was dripping down the boy's face.

"Sir, sir!" Karpushka's high, thin voice

broke in. "Why don't you let him sing a song instead? He's too much of a silly fool to tell us a story!"

"Shut up, Karpushka. He has to tell us a story first. Now, my boy, do as you are told!"

"I don't know any stories."

"What do you mean, you don't know any stories? You know how to steal! How does the Eighth Commandment go?"

"Why are you asking me, sir? How should I know? I swear, we only took one apple, and we took it off the ground!"

"Tell me a story!"

Karpushka began to gather the branches of a thorny bush. The boy knew very well why the thorns were being gathered. Trifon Semyonovich had beautiful ways of taking the law into his own hands. If he found thieves, he sometimes shut them up in a dark room for a day. Or sometimes he beat them with thorns, or took all their clothes and sent them away naked.

Is this news to you? There are people for whom such acts are as common and ordinary as a farm wagon. Gregory looked at the thorny branches out of the corner of his eyes. He was sweating, coughing, and blowing his nose every so often. But now he began to make up a tale. It was about the days when the Russian knights cut down evil monsters and married beautiful ladies. Trifon Semyonovich stood there listening. He never took his eyes from the storyteller.

"That's enough!" he said as the boy's story became too silly. "You are good at telling tales, but you are even better at stealing. And now, my pretty one—" He turned to the girl. "Say the Lord's Prayer."

The pretty one turned red. In a whisper, she said the Lord's Prayer.

"Now I want you to say the Eighth Commandment."

"You think we took a lot of apples, don't you?" the boy said. "You don't believe me at all."

"It's a sad thing, my dears, that you don't know the Eighth Commandment. I'll have to give you a lesson. Did he teach you to steal, my beauty? Why so silent, my little one? You have to answer! Speak! If you keep your mouth shut, that means you agree with me. And now, my pretty, I'll have to ask you to do something. Give your sweetheart a beating for teaching you to steal!"

"I won't!" the girl whispered.

"Oh, just beat him a little bit! He is a fool—he has to be taught a lesson! Give him a beating, my dear. You don't want to? Then I'll have to order Karpushka to give *you* a taste of the thorns. You still don't want to?"

"No, I don't!"

"Karpushka, come here!"

At that moment the girl flew at the boy. She gave him a box on the ears. The boy smiled stupidly, but tears came to his eyes.

"Wonderful, my dear! Now pull his hair out! Go at it, my darling! You don't want to? Karpushka, come here with the thorns!"

The girl grabbed at her sweetheart's hair.

"Don't stand still! Make it hurt! Pull harder!"

The girl really began to pull at her sweetheart's hair. Karpushka roared with joy.

"That is quite enough now!" Trifon Semyonovich said. "Thank you, my dear. You gave a thief what was coming to him. And now," he turned to the boy, "you must teach your girlfriend a lesson. She gave it to you. Now you must give it to her!"

"How could you think of such a thing? Why must I beat her?"

"Why? Well, she gave you a beating, didn't she? Now beat her! It will do her a lot of good! You don't want to? Well, it won't help you! Karpushka, bring the thorns!"

The boy spit on the ground and coughed. Then he grabbed his sweetheart's hair in his hands. He began to punish her. Before long, he became carried away. He forgot he was beating his sweetheart. He thought he was beating Trifon Semyonovich. The girl was screaming at the top of her voice. He kept on beating her for a long time.

I don't know how this story would ever have come to an end if someone had not come along. It was Trifon Semyonovich's charming daughter who had appeared from behind the bushes.

"Papa, come and have tea!" she called. When she saw what was happening, she laughed loudly.

"Stop! That is enough!" said Trifon Semyonovich. "You may go now, my dears. Good-bye! I'll send you some little apples for the wedding."

And Trifon Semyonovich bowed to the couple.

The boy and girl straightened their clothing and went away. The boy went to the right. The girl went to the left. To this day they have never seen each other again. If the daughter had not suddenly appeared, they would probably both have been whipped with thorns. This is how Trifon Semyonovich has fun in his old age.

His family is not much better than he is. His daughters like to sew onions into the caps of visitors whom they believe "belong to the lower class." They also write "Fool" on the backs of those whom they think are beneath them.

Trifon Semyonovich's son outdid his father last winter. With the help of Karpushka, he rubbed a neighbor's gates with tar. He did this because the man would not give him a wolf cub. Also, the neighbor was thought to have warned his daughters against taking candy and cakes from the son.

After this, call Trifon Semyonovich—Trifon Semyonovich.

Thinking About
the Stories

The Bet

1. An author builds the plot around the conflict in a story. In this story, what forces or characters are struggling against each other? How is the conflict finally resolved?

2. Who is the main character in this story? Who are one or two of the minor characters? Describe each of these characters in one or two sentences.

3. What period of time is covered in this story—an hour, a week, several years? What role, if any, does time play in the story?

Gooseberries

1. Compare and contrast at least two characters in this story. In what ways are they alike? In what ways are they different?

2. Many stories are meant to teach a lesson of some kind. Is the author trying to make a point in this story? What is it?

3. All stories fit into one or more categories. Is this story serious or funny? Would you call it an adventure, a love story, or a mystery? Is it a character study? Or is it simply a picture the author has painted of a certain time and place? Explain your thinking.

The Little Apples

1. Which character in this story do you most admire? Why? Which character do you like the least?

2. The plot is the series of events that takes place in a story. Usually, story events are linked in some way. Can you name an event in this story that was the cause of a later event?

3. Suppose this story had a completely different outcome. Can you think of another effective ending for this story?

Thinking About
the Book

1. Choose your favorite illustration in this book. Use this picture as a springboard to write a new story. Give the characters different names. Begin your story with something they are saying or thinking.

2. Compare the stories in this book. Which was the most interesting? Why? In what ways were they alike? In what ways different?

3. Good writers usually write about what they know best. If you wrote a story, what kind of characters would you create? What would be the setting?